30 Days of F

30 Days of Forgiveness

Copyright 2015 to Jeri Massi

All rights reserved. No part of this book may be reproduced or transmitted in any form or by any means, electronic or mechanical, including photocopying, recording, or by any information storage and retrieval system, without written permission from the publisher. For information, contact Jupiter Rising Books.

Forward

30 Days of Forgiveness is the eighth book in the Year of Renewal series, a collection of 12 daily devotional books, each book suited for one month of readings. The goal of this series is to de-educate and re-educate former Christian Fundamentalists on the essential concepts of the Christian faith.

These monthly devotionals are based on a spiraling curriculum. Certain ideas come back again and again and are revisited as the reader progresses through the series. Because of this structure, certain passages are repeated from time to time in the series, with the goal of entrenching them firmly in the reader's mind.

As you pursue your faith, I hope that you find these books helpful.

Jeri Massi

Day One: For thou, Lord, art good, and ready to forgive; and plenteous in mercy unto all them that call upon thee. Psalms 86:5

Psalm 86 is a direct, unadorned prayer to God. Other passages written by David are poetic, adorned with formal structure and imagery. But Psalm 86 is the prayer for mercy, preservation, and forgiveness. In his humility before God, David does not attempt artistry. His plight, as he recounts, is that he is poor and needy (v. 1) and that the proud have risen against him and sought his soul (v. 14).

David gives no account of the occasion for writing this Psalm. It is called "a prayer of David," and the reader can assume that he prayed this prayer more than once. But from the context of the Psalm, two things are possible: First, that David truly feared for his soul because of those who hated him. When he speaks of those who have sought his soul, he may be making reference to those who wished to kill him by assassination.

But it's more likely that David is speaking of his soul in a more profound sense. First, he refers to himself as "poor and needy," that is, a weak man of wretched condition. His word use in the original language indicates a wretched or needy spiritual condition. David is recognizing that he is entirely subject to human frailty. The kingdom over which David ruled regarded him as a mighty man of valor, the captain over a squad of men who performed great feats of warfare. And yet David openly and penitently calls himself weak, prone to sin, and needy of God's protection.

In the Scripture, David frequently and openly recognizes his propensity to sin. And those who hate him may be those who would tempt David to sin, and to sin all the way to his death. As a ruler, David had to be wise and restrained. He was always vulnerable to accusation and was always at risk for downfall by his own foolishness. He had flatterers and deceivers in his own court. The safest way to bring David down was to seduce him or trick him into bringing himself down by sinning against God and shaming the glory of Israel. The downfall David fears from those who "sought after his soul" in verse 14 of this Psalm may have been far more shameful, deadly, and humiliating than just a blow from a sword or club.

But before these enemies, David prays for God's mercy, for God's preservation, and for God's forgiveness. And David does not base his pleas upon his own efforts. He never says he tried his best. He never says he deserves mercy because of his great deeds. He never pleads his crown. The basis of David's hope for forgiveness is God's goodness, not his own: He writes, "Thou, Lord, art good and ready to forgive; and plenteous on mercy unto all that call upon thee." His hope is in the character and nature of God, which is ready to hear the cry of the repentant.

David's hope is our hope. We all need forgiveness, and when we call upon God, forsaking all our own claims, and plead with Him based on His mercy and graciousness to sinners, we find that same God of whom David said in verse 15 of this Psalm, "a God full of compassion, and gracious, longsuffering, and plenteous in mercy and truth."

Day Two: Yet it pleased the LORD to bruise him; he hath put him to grief: when thou shalt make his soul an offering for sin, he shall see his seed, he shall prolong his days, and the pleasure of the LORD shall prosper in his hand."
Isaiah chapter 53:10

Many preachers mistakenly tell people that as the Lord Jesus hung on the Cross, He was tormented by seeing every sin that every one of His people would ever commit, those sins for which He suffered and grieved, and for which He died.

This is not true, if we go by the strict Biblical account. The only thing that made the Lord Jesus cry out upon the Cross was the moment of agony when God turned away from Him, an action caused by Jesus taking our sin upon Himself. But what the Lord Jesus saw, and what sustained Him in His agony, was nothing less than the great victory of the reconciliation He was accomplishing. He did not see our sin; He saw the perfection of His work in us.

Today's verse contains a startling word choice: "it pleased the Lord to bruise him." In this prophecy of Christ the suffering servant, Isaiah faithfully records that God was happy to wound His Son for our sakes. God made the Son of God the head of His people, and God struck our shepherd with our punishment, vindicating His own righteousness with the just punishment of sin. Zechariah also predicted that God would smite the shepherd, His own companion (Zechariah 13:7), a passage that the Lord Jesus also quoted in reference to His own death.

But Christ, rejected of God as He took on our guilt, still ended His earthly life with a triumphant shout: "It is finished!" which is more correctly translated, "It is accomplished!" Christ was not declaring that His life was over, but that His mission was complete. He had purchased us with His blood; He had suffered unto death for His own. As Isaiah predicted, "He shall see His seed."

Christ knew that His people would be given to Him, redeemed by His blood.

God, though wrathful with the Son of God upon the Cross, indicated by that very wrath as He turned away that Christ had truly taken our sin upon Himself. Christ was rejected as He became sin, and in that moment, our acceptance with God was forever won. Christ was slain; the wrath of God was then appeased. Christ purchased a people to glorify His name.

The sins of His own people never daunted the Lord Jesus Christ from doing exactly what He set out to do. He knew from the start what we are. The tremendous stink of humanity, our corruption, disease, death, lies, adulteries, betrayal, name calling, theft----everything, had been around Him all His life while on earth. He was fully purposed to take all of that upon Himself and bear our sins away.

Isaiah also foretells that what comforted the Savior as He hung between heaven and earth was that He would see His seed---us, His people, no longer doomed to be bound in sin, no longer slaves to what we are by nature. He knew that the deliverance would take place. He knew that even though He was slain under wrath, that under the favor of God He would prolong His days, as Isaiah wrote in this passage: our king. We had been won by His labors into eternal fellowship with God. Jesus Christ has made provision to forgive His people, and to forgive them abundantly.

Day Three: Who is a God like unto thee, that pardoneth iniquity, and passeth by the transgression of the remnant of his heritage? He retaineth not his anger for ever, because He delighteth in mercy.
Micah 7:18

Micah lived during a time of outward social propriety and secret depravity. In chapter seven of his prophecy, he laments that the righteous are like single grapes found scattered in a field by the gleaners. There are not enough righteous people to form a cluster, like grapes when they are plentiful (vv 1 and 2). He declares that the men of noble office are all asking for a reward: bribe takers who have the office of executing God's Word (v. 3) Even the most sacred of human relationships: friend to friend, child to parent, husband to wife, are filled with envy, backbiting, and treachery. No one is to be trusted.

Upon close inspection, Micah realizes that there is sin within himself. He is no better than his peers. But he resolves to trust the Lord during a time of God's chastening. While the godless men and women around him, even those who hold high religious office, assume themselves to be beyond reproach and safe in their sin, Micah throws himself upon God. First, he warns his adversaries that even in the darkness of present suffering and the chastening hand of God, that God is His light. He stands fast in accepting God's chastening and he declares, "I will bear the indignation of the LORD, because I have sinned against him, until he plead my cause, and execute judgment for me: he will bring me forth to the light, [and] I shall behold his righteousness. (Micah 7:9).

Micah recognizes that a loving God will at times sternly rebuke those who love Him for their sins. But he also understands that this chastening is not damnation from God. Quite the opposite. In a time of suffering reproach from God, he knows full well that even this trial is God's way of bringing him close enough to see the brightness of God's light and to behold God's righteousness, a place of honor with God, intimate friendship, and security. God intends that His Beloved people will know Him and delight in Him, and even sorrow is His means to enlighten us with all the good He intends for us.

Thus, recognizing his own sinfulness and realizing that God's plan is to bless him with fellowship with God forever, Micah breaks into praise of God and concludes with this great hope for all who trust in God to forgive their sins: "He will have compassion upon us; he will subdue our iniquities; and thou wilt cast all their sins into the depths of the sea" (Micah 7:19). Micah humbled himself before God's chastening and he hoped in God, knowing that God will subdue our sins by His power, and not our own.

Day Four: Let the wicked forsake his way, and the unrighteous man his thoughts: and let him return unto the LORD, and he will have mercy upon him; and to our God, for he will abundantly pardon.
Isaiah 55:7

Through the prophet Isaiah in the 55th chapter of his book, God extends a gracious invitation: In comparing the riches of mercy that He has to offer them to the short-lived pleasures of their pride, He calls upon the people to buy wine and milk without money and without price. He urges them to cease from their labor, to stop toiling for things that do not satisfy them. Isaiah's countrymen in his day lived under the same delusions as many of the religious people of our day: they believed that there is a level of prosperity and tamed worldliness that everybody should strive to attain. Isaiah lived in an outwardly prosperous, religious culture. Religion was a big business and made up a significant part of society and social life. Yet it was all merely external, all unfulfilling, all aimed at worldly goals, all done in alienation from God, even though it was all done in His name. But no matter how well dressed this worldliness was in crowns and robes and high office, and no matter how ornamented with religious language and phrasing, it was utterly corrupt.

For behind the front of religious devotion, there was injustice: a lust for money that caused people to break the Sabbath, demand hard labor from the poor, use slavery against their own people, and oppress the helpless. Again and again in the book of Isaiah, God cites his grievances against the false religious show of the people, And in chapter 55, not far from the end of the book, He still invites them to come and be forgiven.

The commentator Matthew Henry writes that repentance has two phases, as today's verse indicates. First, to turn from sin. He writes, "We must alter our judgments concerning persons and things, dislodge the corrupt imaginations and quit the vain pretenses under which an unsanctified heart shelters itself." And second, to repent is to *return to the Lord;* to return to him as our God, the one whose rule over us is just and necessary; and it is to turn to Him as our source of righteousness, our righteous covering and our means of living righteously.

God's invitation shows His prompt readiness to fulfill our need of Him for imputed and integrated righteousness. He greets sinners with mercy and with abundant pardon. The Hebrew word for mercy in this passage, racham, is a word for a tender compassion, a compassionate pity. God is ready to take up the repentant sinner as a mother takes up an ailing or injured child and make everything all right again. He is speaking of Himself as a caregiver to a needy and pained soul; He is the one who will effect the cure.

God's mindset is to pardon the sinner. And so whatever we do wrong in this life, the moment we realize that our actions are offensive, instead of running from God, we must run to Him. This is what God wants from us: not the vestments and money and grandeur of a civil, conservative, but corrupt religious society, but rather, the humble call from sinners, the prayer of repentance, a heart that loathes its sin, and souls that hope in Him. God is Holy and righteous, but He also identifies Himself as the God who forgives and shows mercy to sinners.

Day Five: If my people, which are called by my name, shall humble themselves, and pray, and seek my face, and turn from their wicked ways; then will I hear from heaven, and will forgive their sin, and will heal their land.
Second Chronicles 7:14

In Second Chronicles, the young King Solomon built the House of God. He crowned this great achievement of architecture and splendor with a 14 day feast and prayer of supplication and dedication to God. In his prayer, he begged God to put His presence in the temple, and to make the temple a place of forgiveness and justice. He laid out before God every possible condition of judgment that God might bring forth against the people if they were disobedient, and he asked God in each situation to forgive the people if they should repent. He even included a plea for God's mercy to strangers to Israel, who might hear of the goodness and justice of Jehovah and would therefore come to the temple to see it for themselves and call upon God. And He asked God, for the sake of God's name, to hear them.

In Chapter seven, God answers Solomon's prayers, first with fire from heaven that consumed the offerings. And then the Lord filled the temple with His glory. But later, after the seven days of dedication and seven days of feasting were finished, the Lord appeared to Solomon and gave him this promise, found in today's Scripture passage. For every eventuality that Solomon had thought of, God assured him of forgiveness if the people would forsake sin and repent.

Solomon had built a place of majesty for God's name, but he understood that the magnificence of God's name is bound up in His willingness and power to forgive. What validated the temple as the place where God's presence dwelled was not the gold, the ivory and the precious stones that adorned it, but the forgiveness and the justice forever associated with that place.

The Lord Jesus, in John chapter 2, referred to Himself as a temple. And the Lord Jesus Christ did bring the temple to life, for He was filled with the glory of God. John wrote of Him, "we beheld his glory, the glory as of the only begotten of the Father, full of grace and truth. " (John 1:14).

And the Lord Jesus, after the model of forgiveness for which Solomon prayed, forgave sins and corrected the corrupt religious instruction of His day, restoring justice. The Lord Jesus, as the living temple of God, didn't have to come in the splendor of the manmade temple in order to refer to Himself as a temple. He came, forgiving sinners and establishing justice. And by forgiveness and justice, He proved that the glory of the temple, the residence of God, rested on Him.

Day Six: And hearken thou to the supplication of thy servant, and of thy people Israel, when they shall pray toward this place: and hear thou in heaven thy dwelling place: and when thou hearest, forgive.
First Kings chapter 8:30

Today's passage shows us the heart of Solomon's prayer at the dedication of the temple. From the time that God led His people out of Egypt, He had promised that He would bring them into their own Land and dwell among them. God gave to His People the Ark of the Covenant, an ensign of His presence, the representation of His sacred relationship with them as His chosen people.

Where once the Ark had resided in a tabernacle, it was the hope of kings to build a temple as a place to house the Ark, in honor. Toward this end, King David had worked, in preparing materials for the temple. And David's son Solomon brought the plans of his father and the greatest architects in the region to execution. He built a magnificent temple to serve as the residence where God could dwell, if God would condescend to maintain His presence among His People. For, as Solomon confessed in verse 15 of today's chapter, the heaven, and heaven of heavens cannot contain God. Only by God's decree could some manifestation of His presence be made to dwell among His people.

Furthermore, Solomon prayed a lengthy prayer of supplication, on his knees before God and before all the nation, asking God to make His house a house of forgiveness. For Solomon understood what many neglect. If God dwells among us, right at hand, we must beg for Him to come with a mindset of forgiveness for human sin.

Otherwise, the presence of God would be a terror to us, a constant sentence of death.

The presence of God among sinners can be a terror to them, a sentence of eternal punishment. Isaiah himself, godly man that he was, cried out in terror when he saw God, saying "Woe is me! for I am undone; because I am a man of unclean lips, and I dwell in the midst of a people of unclean lips: for mine eyes have seen the King, the LORD of hosts" (Isaiah 6:5). The presence of God is a terrifying experience for sinners, unless God makes it bearable for them.

And so Solomon wisely prayed for God to come with forgiveness and justice, so that His presence would be the hope and delight for all who would come seeking His pardon. God, as we have seen previously, answered Solomon's prayer by the consuming fire, by the presence of His glory in the temple, and by granting Solomon a vision in which God specifically promised His forgiveness and justice.

Similarly, the Lord Jesus, when He came as the living temple of God, directly said that "God sent not his Son into the world to condemn the world; but that the world through him might be saved." Christ came, the ultimate fulfillment of God's promise to dwell among His people, with forgiveness for the repentant. We see from His life and death that those who were condemned already hated Him and ultimately killed Him. But those who loved Him were given His forgiveness and His favor. Christ has made us acceptable with God, so that we can enjoy the peace and acceptance of God With Us.

Day Seven: If we confess our sins, he is faithful and just to forgive us our sins, and to cleanse us from all unrighteousness.
First John 1:9

Our struggles with sin never take our Savior by surprise. His continuing work on our behalf is to bring us into conformity with His righteousness. And our Master is not given to frustration, despair, or weariness. Just as we are prone to sin, so Christ is prone to Mercy and Grace. Our inborn natures lead us one way; but His nature leads Him another. The relationship of Christ to His People includes three steadfast, unchanging responsibilities that He has put upon Himself for our sakes:

First, Christ is being faithful to the will of the Father and to His own work on the Cross to forgive us. We don't impose on Him or frustrate His purposes when we ask His forgiveness. His willingness to forgive us rests upon His dedication to conform us to His image. He has entered a covenant relationship with us, in which we have no power and He has all the power and authority. God created that covenant of salvation and reconciliation, and Christ fulfills its requirements. Therefore He is fulfilling His mission when He forgives us.

Second, Christ is just to forgive us. In the covenant relationship that He has fulfilled, the terms are that we are unrighteous by nature, and He is all our righteousness. The Savior who boldly declared that He came to save sinners and not the righteous would be proved untrue if He should fail to forgive those who come to Him for forgiveness. By His righteous nature, He cannot turn us away when we repent and ask Him to forgive us, because He has declared that He is our salvation, and God vindicated this claim when God raised Him from the dead. Furthermore, neither God the Son nor God the Father have any inclination to forsake us when we sin. God the Father accepted the offering of His Son. To reject one of the people for whom Christ atoned would be to reject what His Son did on the Cross. If Christ were to reject one of His own, then He would be rejecting His own work on our behalf. That's not possible. As Ephesians chapter one tells us, our salvation was mapped out before time began, and nothing is so sure as the sureness of our salvation. Forgiving those who are in Christ is just and right for God to do, so have no fear on that account. Place your hope in God's forgiveness, and you will not be disappointed.

Finally, Christ is faithful and just to cleanse us from all unrighteousness. In this life, we are not delivered from the presence of sin in us. Our sinful nature is not eliminated as long as we remain in our flesh. God has been pleased to make our transformation a more gradual process that requires constant cleansing from Christ while we live on this earth. Our Savior's faithfulness to us is glorified when we turn to Him for cleansing. He does not turn us away. If we expect to stop being sinners, we will be disappointed, for the life of the Christian has to be lived by faith in the One who works in us. But when we come to Him, expecting Him to be our righteousness and forgive us, we are not disappointed.

Yes, we will come to Christ again tomorrow and the next day and the day after, but the Lord Jesus is faithful and just. He works in us day to day to conform us to His image.

Day Eight: It may be that the house of Judah will hear all the evil which I purpose to do unto them; that they may return every man from his evil way; that I may forgive their iniquity and their sin.
Jeremiah 36:3

God extends gracious invitations to sinners to repent, and He uses kindness and promises to entice their hearts. But the Lord also promises justice against wickedness. Sin has fatal consequences, and God delivers punishment against transgressors. And yet He forthrightly declares that He does not take pleasure in the death of the wicked, but rather delights in their repentance (Ezekiel 33:11). The Lord Jesus confirmed this attitude of God the Father when He said that there is joy in the presence of the angels of God over one sinner that repents (Luke 15:10).

And yet God does draw a boundary. There does come a point when God executes His wrath against sin. In Amos chapter four, God lists the punishments He has executed against Israel because they have trampled over the poor and helpless. He directly takes responsibility for famine, for drought, for pestilence, for disease, for war, for catastrophe against a wicked society that claimed to know Him, and still they would not repent. And God declares in that sobering chapter that He will destroy them. He will bring them to eternal judgment, where they will see him face to face (Amos 4:12).

God in His mercy saves sinners. God also destroys sinners. But He provides for them to understand their sin and transgressions. In today's passage, God directs the prophet Jeremiah to make a record of God's charges against Israel and Judah. Now, the people already had the Law. And the Law plainly declares that God would punish

His people if they should embrace evil. These were not sinners sinning in ignorance. The religious leaders of Jeremiah's day paid lip service to the Law and to God, but they twisted God's Word and turned it, and used it to oppress others and make themselves rich and powerful.

God's direction to Jeremiah, fearful as His words are, is a gracious directive. For before He brings wrath down upon a people who knowingly have corrupted His sacred words, He commands that they should be warned again, in no uncertain terms. God directs that this final warning is to be written and read aloud in public, for all to hear and know.

Some people, when they suffer unjustly, often ask where God is. But God is slow to bring His wrath down upon His creatures. He does give man time to repent. Still, as we see in the book of Jeremiah, that after years of oppressing the innocent and the poor, and even afflicting the prophet himself, King Zedekiah was captured by his enemies. His sons were killed in front of him; his eyes were put out, and he was thrown into a foreign prison, to die alone there, in darkness. All of the wealthy and powerful elite were also executed by the Babylonian king. The patience of God is not to be taken for granted. He does bring His wrath down upon those who willfully transgress, and He counts sins against the poor and needy as sins against Him. It is not for nothing that David and many other prophets urge us to worship God, to love Him, and to fear Him. As David writes in Psalm 103:13, "Like as a father pitieth [his] children, [so] the LORD pitieth them that fear him. " Fearing God and knowing that He does punish sin is a means of living by faith and repentance in Him.

Day Nine: For I say unto you, That except your righteousness shall exceed the righteousness of the scribes and Pharisees, ye shall in no case enter into the kingdom of heaven.
Matthew 5:20

The Lord Jesus, having just taught the Beatitudes and the estate of the Blessed upon this earth, undoubtedly dismayed His listeners when, after speaking of such hope for the lowly and meek, He articulated this mandate of the Law and made it a bedrock of His teachings. Indeed, if we consult this passage of Matthew, we see that the Lord follows this statement with a series of warnings that shows that every human being, including the Pharisees, is not able to fulfill the law and the demand for perfection. The scribes and Pharisees allowed divorce as the husband's prerogative, but the Lord Jesus condemned it. The scribes and Pharisees articulated many infractions about the *committing* of sin, but the Lord Jesus declared that even deliberately *contemplating* sin and harboring wicked thoughts of either lust or hatred was sin.

In fact, after the gracious words of the first part of the Sermon on the Mount, this section of the Sermon is frightening. All mankind is in a horrible plight, for nobody's righteousness can meet the standard set by Scripture, which was the standard that the Lord Jesus was upholding: perfect righteousness.

Now, we know from the full canon of Scripture that the Lord Jesus quickly forgave repentant sinners. In the parable of the Publican and the Pharisee, the Lord declares the Publican justified: that is, declared righteous, after his sorrow and remorse before God. On the Cross itself, the

Lord guaranteed to a dying thief that they would be together that very day in Paradise.

There are two conclusions to draw from Christ's directive in this passage. First, the religion of the scribes and Pharisees, which the Jews at that time thought was the pinnacle of true religion, was entirely based on externals. And Christ would have none of it. He does not demand a show of piety, but rather true piety within the human heart. In many ways, Christ's sermon was a direct deconstruction of the Pharisees' religion, based on the teachings of the Torah and the Prophets. The religion of God is, and always has been, based upon a humble and contrite heart before God, a life of running to Him openly for forgiveness and cleansing, of taking our griefs and injuries to Him and committing them into His Hand. The scribes and Pharisees had built a religion of ceremony and strict external observances, but their hearts were proud and filled with the images of their own righteousness.

Second, Christ is obviously stating an impossible case for all of mankind. Even the scribes and Pharisees were not righteous enough by their own works to merit the kingdom of heaven. All of mankind shares the same plight before God. We cannot meet His standard. If God does not graciously forgive us and declare us righteous, we are all lost. And this statement has been anticipated in this same sermon by the Lord's promise that whoever hunger and thirsts for righteousness shall be filled. This is our comfort. Even the Old Testament prophets understood that only God could supply our missing righteousness, and Jeremiah called God "Jehovah Tsidkenu," the Lord our Righteousness. Christ honestly shows us our plight of sinfulness, but He comforts us with the promise that when we come hungering and thirsting for righteousness, He is our righteousness. He has the power to forgive our sins and to be our righteousness.

Day Ten: But that ye may know that the Son of man hath power on earth to forgive sins, (then saith he to the sick of the palsy,) Arise, take up thy bed, and go unto thine house. And he arose, and departed to his house.
Matthew 9:6-7

Having re-established the tenets of true religion in the Sermon on the Mount in Matthew chapters 5 through 7, the Lord Jesus validated His authority before His disciples and before the crowds that followed Him by a series of miracles that are documented in Matthew chapter 8. All of His words and actions were unassailable. The Sermon on the Mount is actually a second giving of the same Law given to Moses, expounded to show God's gracious intent to sinners. The scribes and Pharisees did not dare wrestle the Scripture with Him, for they knew He could beat them at their own game. They hated what He taught, as all apostates hate it when the Word of God is taken out of their own hands and clearly taught for what it actually says, instead of being presented with the false teachings they have imposed upon it.

And so the only strategy that the apostate teachers of the nation could fall back on was that of accusation. And so they were a part of the multitude following the Lord Jesus, and they carefully watched Him to find some fault with Him. And Christ gave them the rope necessary for them to hang themselves. In the ninth chapter of Matthew, when the man with the debilitating palsy was brought before Him, Christ asks no questions of the man and simply declares, "Thy sins be forgiven thee." It was an audacious promise, and one from which Christ gave Himself no loopholes. Even a Pharisee could make some type of promise about forgiveness if he knew that a person had performed all the right rituals and observed the Law and offered the proper sacrifices. But Christ does not test this child of God His with questions. He simply forgives him outright: a clear claim to His authority to act as God.

This was what the scribes had been waiting for. None of them spoke, but they satisfied themselves with the realization that they had found the accusation that they could bring against Christ. And they were all witnesses to it. He had claimed the authority of God in forgiving sin, and He had done so very clearly.

And so the Lord Jesus directly addresses them, and in His words, He makes clear to them, and to everybody else who stood in the crowd, that He knew their thoughts. He sets an easy question for them: which is easier, to say that a person's sins are forgiven, or to command that he get up and walk? Again, He is clearly claiming His authority in this passage. Only God can miraculously heal an incurable affliction, just as only God can forgive sin. So if the Lord Jesus can do the one, He can do the other; and then, as today's text gives us, He healed the man, and the poor man, no longer afflicted, took up his bed and went home. Thus, Christ's accusers were silenced.

And our hope is this man's hope. We are afflicted, bound, and made powerless by sin. But the Lord Jesus has that authority to release us from our bonds and our affliction. In Him, we have the forgiveness of our sins, the restorations of our minds from slavery to envy and lust, to minds of faith and hope in God. Christ has the authority to forgive our sin, and, as with this man, He directly forgives those who come to Him.

Day Eleven: Blessed are the poor in spirit: for theirs is the kingdom of heaven.
Matthew 5:3

The Beatitudes are not directly promises on HOW to be blessed by working harder to be good. They are declarations of who IS blessed. The word "if" never appears among them. Christ does not say, "If you are poor enough in spirit, you will inherit the Kingdom of heaven." It's not a recipe. It's not a challenge. Christ framed the Beatitudes as observation, a commentary on who is Blessed. So Christ says, "Blessed ARE the poor in spirit, etc." There exists a Blessed People of God, and Christ is describing them.

When Christ said "Blessed are the poor in spirit," He deliberately chose a word that means utterly destitute. This is not the poverty of those who live hand to mouth by what they earn. Even deeper into poverty! This word is used for those entirely dependent on alms. This word describes those who do not earn because they cannot earn. They have nothing to claim as their own. Everything they wear and everything they eat is given to them.

To be this poor in spirit is to have nothing to bring before God as a claim. Those who are poor in spirit hold their hands out to God, empty, needing Him to fill them. The best example of a man poor in spirit is the publican in Luke 18:13 "And the publican, standing afar off, would not lift up so much as his eyes unto heaven, but smote upon his breast, saying, God be merciful to me a sinner."

If you examine the Greek for this verse, you discover that the Publican, standing in the temple where the offerings were slaughtered, is actually saying, "Be propitiated" or

"Be reconciled." His prayer is the cry of a person who knows he cannot reconcile himself to God by his own merit but trusts that God will look upon the Atonement of blood and be reconciled to Him.

When Christ spoke of this pleading Publican, He declared that this humble man returned home justified, "declared righteous." How blessed is the person who has no merit to claim before God! To be contrite before God and too heart sore over sin to boast before Him is a demonstration of the blessed estate of the Christian, not finding any confidence in the flesh. And to these people, Christ declares, comes the kingdom of heaven. Heed the warning of Matthew 7:21-22, where those who plead their good works at the judgment are condemned by God. The Kingdom is given to repentant sinners.

When Christ tells us "theirs is the kingdom of heaven," the word choice is crucial, for the word for kingdom, means both the rulership and the territory. Remember, we shall reign with Christ (Rev 20:6). He will put His Blessed People on thrones. Those who openly declare to God that they have nothing to count on but His mercy are accepted as royalty into His kingdom.

Day Twelve: Blessed are they that mourn: for they shall be comforted.
Matthew 5:4

The people whom God has chosen to bless are those who bewail their condition. The type of mourning Christ describes is not a soft sorrow, but a display of sorrow not able to be hidden. People who mourn this way are grief stricken.

In the day that Christ taught us face to face, religious leaders took comfort in their material prosperity, and they considered health, wealth, and strong family ties a sign of blessing from God. They assured themselves that by virtue of their exalted positions in their religious society, that they had peace with God. To maintain an undisturbed, untroubled, sanctimonious expression was part of their externalized religion. Suffering grief was a sign to them that God had deserted a person and was punishing him for sins.

At the time of John the Baptist and Christ, a lot of people were fearful that the words of the prophet Isaiah were being fulfilled: Israel would be destroyed and yet Israel would be restored. When John baptized, he baptized after the commission given in Isaiah 1:16, for the time had come for Israel to be purged, as Isaiah predicted would happen. And many people repented and fearfully and mournfully expected to see God carry out His decree in Isaiah 1:25-31. They believed the time was on them when Zion would be redeemed with judgment: her converts would be purified, her transgressors destroyed.

A time of great change was at hand. The Kingdom was coming in, as both John and Christ preached. Thus, people mourned openly for their sin. Christ asserts to them that their condition is not indicative of God's wrath upon them, but His mercy. How happy is the person who dreads and respects the righteousness of God so much that he weeps over his own sin! After all, many people fail to be righteous and don't mourn. Many people fail to be righteous but insist that they are righteous. Many people fail to be righteous and dare to mock those who mourn their sin.

When Christ speaks of the comfort that will be given, He uses a future tense verb, a verb that indicates definite fact. The people who mourn shall receive a comforter, the "parakaleo". This is the Person who comes alongside us and both comforts and teaches us. We would consider such a Person to be an older, wiser Friend. He takes our part, and yet He can also explain things to us and make things right for us. The root form of this word can also be used to indicate a change for the better: a happier estate. This Comforter who helps us gives us a happier lot.

Christ had to ascend to take on the role of our High Priest. At the time that He spoke, He offered His good will, His instruction, His mercies to those He met, but the true fulfillment came after He died and rose again. To this day, Christ is the Comforter who comes alongside us to console us, to teach us, to change our estate and bring us into peace with God, to cause us to share in His rich estate of Sonship and acceptance. He is our Comforter. Christ's comfort is for the people who mourn over what they are before God, in such a way that is open and transparent. They are the blessed people of God.

Day Thirteen: Blessed are the meek: for they shall inherit the earth.
Matthew 5:5

Soldiers, kings, and the wealthy inherit the earth. At least, that's the way that the world thinks. Everybody, sooner or later, has to set aside ideals to get ahead in this world. A person has to look out for "Number One." But the Lord Jesus taught that the ultimate ownership of the land will be given to the meek. But the idea of the Christian who never takes a stand, never speaks up, never defends an ideal or a fellowman has been incorrectly assigned to the idea of being meek. The Lord Jesus condemned the abusive practices of His day, but He lived a life of meekness and humility.

Meekness in the sense that the Lord Jesus was using it, according to Strong's Concordance, is the willingness to accept God's decrees for what they say. Christ's sermon falls hard upon the call of the Lord Jesus to the nation to repent in the previous chapter (Matt. 4:17). God, as Jesus so often demonstrated, was not appeased by sacrifice, by vestments, by fast days, by external piety. God wants the poor in heart, those who do not dare claim their merit before His righteousness. He wants those who mourn over their sin and no longer hide behind pretenses of external religion. He claims those who hear His Word and accept His way of salvation, not demanding their own way.

How often do we hear people reject the Gospel when they say, "I can't believe in a God who condemns people to Hell" or "I believe in a God who accepts all religions". These are people who are not meek; they place demands on God, telling Him what He must be before they condescend to submit to Him. And if you think their arrogance is alarming (or even funny), recall to mind the people who think they are right with God because they wear certain clothing or have been baptized a certain way or keep the Sabbath or don't go to movies or have modernized their church music. These people are also putting demands on God, insisting that they have some sort of "edge" or higher standing than others whom God has justified by the Blood of His Son Jesus Christ!

Job suffered many things from the decree of God, though God acknowledged that Job was innocent. And Job himself, near the end of his story, blamed God and indicted Him as not being righteous in apportioning suffering to Job. Yet Job, when he saw God face to face, even before he fully understood God's lesson to him, humbly repented and accepted God's will. He declared, "I know that thou canst do every thing, and that no thought can be withholden from thee….I have heard of thee by the hearing of the ear: but now mine eye seeth thee. Wherefore I abhor myself, and repent in dust and ashes" (42:2-6).

And Job, a godly man in spite of his frail flesh, was restored by God to meekness when he saw God. It's this astounding meekness that shows the grace of God. The repentant sinner does not boast before God; mourns over the presence, corruption, and weight of his sin without pretense; and accepts God's authority over him. And the person who meekly accepts God's rulership will one day inherit the earth. The person who subjects himself to the reign of Christ, repenting and believing in Him, will one day reign with Christ, as Christ foretold. For Christ makes His Beloved people kings and priests with God (Rev 1:6).

Day Fourteen: But I say unto you, Love your enemies, bless them that curse you, do good to them that hate you, and pray for them which despitefully use you, and persecute you; That ye may be the children of your Father which is in heaven: for he maketh his sun to rise on the evil and on the good, and sendeth rain on the just and on the unjust. Matthew 5:44-45

The Lord Jesus' directive on forgiveness are without exception and without apology. But first, because so many of my listeners have been horribly abused by men who hold church office unjustly, it should be clear from the Scripture that forgiveness does not eliminate rebuke, for the Lord taught in Luke chapter 17, verse 3 that we are to rebuke those who wrong us. We are allowed to articulate the wrongs done to us by another person and hand that declaration to the person who as wronged us as a means to be reconciled. But we may not rail against an evil doer, and we may not seek revenge.

Forgiveness does not ignore the reality of evil deeds, nor does it excuse them. For our sakes, the Lord Jesus bore our punishment in order to be the Atonement for our sins. He did not simply ignore our sins. He suffered and died for them, all so that He could forgive us. But forgiveness does place the evil things that others do to us under the loving and patient Hand of God.

In today's passage, forgiveness is based upon the imitation of God and our submission to Him. God in His kindness and patience sends the sun and the rain upon both the evil and the good on this earth. We have reaped the benefit of His patience, for we have come to repentance and faith while God chose to bear with our sins and provide for us to live on the face of the earth. In the same way, as forgiven people, we must bear with the sins of others. We must live in the hope that God will forgive their sins as He forgave ours, and therefore, as Christ directed, we pray for our enemies and speak of them with restraint and care. This does not mean that we lie for them or excuse them, but their wrongs make us grieve, and we seek their best at all times, hoping that the Love that has borne with us will bear with them to their salvation.

Second, forgiving our enemies is our statement to the world, in actions that speak much more loudly than words, that we subject ourselves to God's Will. Yes, criminally evil people must be brought to justice. Yes, fallen elders must be removed from pulpits to protect the flock. The Bible itself mandates these things. But we must deal gently and generously with those who harm us, as an expression of our subjection to God. Even the Lord Jesus carried out this difficult task. Yes, He did rebuke the Pharisees, and He pointed out their evil. At the same time, He ate with them when they would have Him come, and He explained the Scripture to them again and again. He showed tem His grace when He healed sinners. He never denied them His wisdom and the truth of His miracles. Christ often taught the Pharisees, when all they wanted to do was find some pretense to accuse Him. Christ served them, evidencing that he was serving God in humble submission.

Forgiving our enemies as Christ taught: dealing kindly with them and praying for them, is our clearest demonstration that we, poor sinners, have been forgiven by God and live in the hope of that forgiveness.

Day Fifteen: So shall ye say unto Joseph, Forgive, I pray thee now, the trespass of thy brethren, and their sin; for they did unto thee evil: and now, we pray thee, forgive the trespass of the servants of the God of thy father. And Joseph wept when they spake unto him.
Genesis chapter 50:17

In one of the most spiteful and cruel crimes recorded in the Bible, Joseph's brothers dreadfully wronged him when they sold him into slavery as an adolescent. They hated his dreams, which foretold that they would one day bow down to him, and so they sought to bring his dreams to nothing, and they sold him into a life of savage abuse and bondage. Over the ensuing years, Joseph suffered probably about as much as they could have wished: enduring false accusation and years of imprisonment. And yet, for all the malice against him, Joseph continually found favor. And his brothers, for all their freedom and even the promises of God that they expected from their lineage after their own father, could never quite prosper. Until at last, they came begging to their brother for bread, not knowing his identity after all the years that had passed.

In today's passage, we see the guilty fear and abject humility of Joseph's brothers. He had already forgiven them and provided lands and protection for them in Goshen. And yet, with the death of their father, they first entreated Joseph through a mediator, calling upon him to remember their father and to act in kindness, according to his wishes. Then his brothers came to him face to face, calling upon God to Joseph, calling themselves his servants, and actually prostrating themselves before him.

Yet Joseph had not asked for any of this and had been living under the assumption that they knew they were forgiven after his first assurances years earlier. How untroubled is the mind and heart of the person who forgives and rests upon the forgiveness of God. Joseph has no share in the turmoil of his brothers. He loved them and cared for them openly, while they feared to trust his open and kind hearted grace to them.

And when they came, begging mercy a second time, fearful and humble, Joseph wept. It could be that he wept because this was the fulfillment of his dream as a boy, when he dreamed that his brethren would bow down to him. At long last, decades later, he saw that God had carefully appointed his days to come to this point. And now Joseph was mature enough to see God exalted, and not himself, in the fulfillment of his dream. Joseph may have wept because he saw that his brothers still did not understand the comprehensive need every man has for God's mercy, nor the comprehensive mercy God offers to man. For Joseph asks them, "Am I in the place of God?" Clearly, he understood that God alone has the right to take revenge. Joseph was a God-fearing man who did not seize upon opportunities for revenge. He was forgiven, and God had blessed him; and so Joseph forgave his former enemies and blessed them. And finally, Joseph understood that his suffering was part of a greater story: for by him, the offspring of his brothers, and therefore a great nation, was saved.

"Ye thought evil against me;" he tells them, "But God meant it unto good, to bring to pass, as [it is] this day, to save much people alive." And so Joseph demonstrated his submission to God by recognizing that his own suffering had become a means of honoring God and preserving God's people.

Day Sixteen: For if ye forgive men their trespasses, your heavenly Father will also forgive you:
Matthew 6:14

Today's passage begins a section of the Sermon on the Mount that truly defines Christianity and yet is one of its most difficult practices. The Lord Jesus had just given the Lord's prayer, the ideal sample and the text for the prayer that serves as the benchmark for all Christian prayer. Many commentators have noted that the Lord Jesus actually combined many common devotional statements in His prayer. His listeners were familiar with each line of the prayer, as He gave it, until He said "forgive us our debts, as we forgive our debtors". This was new and strange to His audience.

The Jewish religion had come under the guidance and leadership of extremely legalistic men who counted up the sins of others and counted up their own merit. When a man had been wronged, he usually supposed that he had a right to condemn and blame the person who had wronged him. And this practice of looking upon the evils of others was ingrained into their religion, until Christ came and corrected the doctrine of His people.

First, this startling doctrine reminds us of God's respect for forgiveness. Mercy itself, the right to pardon sin, is the Divine prerogative. From the founding of the nation of Israel, when God spoke with Moses, God declared that forgiveness is His executive right, for He said in Exodus 33:19 that He would be gracious to whom He would be gracious, and would shew mercy on whom He would shew mercy. But God's inclination is to pardon, and He has also said that He does not turn away from the humble and contrite heart. As creatures who need forgiveness, we glorify God and testify of our Hope in Him as our sole rescue when we forgive others and exercise that Divine prerogative in His name.

Human beings like to imitate God by amassing power and declaring what others must do, acquiring the right to give orders and to be glorified of men by exercising authority. But God delights in our imitation of Him when we imitate His mercy and pardon and forgive others.

Furthermore, the mindset of the forgiven person is to forgive. The Lord Jesus, in this text, tells His listeners to forgive as a condition of their lives. He uses the Aorist tense in His directive to them, a verb tense that does not exist in English. This tense is used for any action that can happen at any time or any action that has a definite beginning point but continues indefinitely. What the Lord Jesus is saying is that forgiving others must be our mindset, our continual way of life. We must make this a part of our religious devotion, the same as prayer and Scripture reading. But when he refers to God forgiving us, He speaks in the future tense. At this point in His sermon, he is not speaking of the day to day cleansing from sin that we need from God. The Lord is pointing to the expectation of His listeners to be pardoned by God at the gates of heaven.

If we live lives of forgiving others, He is saying, then when we meet God in the future, He will forgive us. And this promise is one at which the flesh stumbles. No human being can keep this dictate of Christ's, just as none of us can refrain from lust or anger. Only in Christ, and by Christ, can His people practice the grace given to them and forgive others. But it is this characteristic that most clearly demonstrates our faith in Christ and Christ the source of our own forgiveness and mercy.

Day Seventeen: But if ye forgive not men their trespasses, neither will your Father forgive your trespasses.
Matthew 6:15

Today's passage is another of those difficult passages that the Lord Jesus handed down in His key Sermon on the Mount. He has comforted us with the promises of the Beatitudes, and He has shown us the readiness of God to tenderly forgive and restore repentant sinners, to feed those who hunger and thirst for righteousness with the Water of Life and the Bread of Life, giving them righteousness. And yet Christ also upholds the rightness and the requirements of the Law given to Moses. We must not only turn from adultery: we may not even lust. We must not only with hold our hands from murder: we may not hold hatred in our hearts. And this most difficult, certainly impossible command and its burden: we must forgive, and if we do not forgive, we will not be forgiven.

There is a certain amount of terror and appropriate humiliation of the human spirit in this command. For we are never allowed to think we have gotten so far in our spiritual lives that we can forget our true condition of needing God's forgiveness. Not one of us gets an exemption from our need of forgiveness and our duty to forgive because we have been forgiven.

Who can keep this decree from Christ? Certainly, it is possible to forgive only if we have received forgiveness and considered how great that mercy is that has spared us. Only the poor in spirit, those who have realized that they are empty handed before God and begged Him for spiritual life, which He gives, can forgive others. Only those who have mourned over their own sin can mourn over the sins of others and have compassion on them.

As in the previous verse, the verb tense for "forgive not," is Aorist tense. It describes an action that can occur at any time: past, present, or future. It also indicates actions that have a starting point but continue indefinitely. This tense indicates that we who profess Christ must have mindsets to forgive, lifestyles of forgiveness. And the verb tense for God's forgiveness in this passage is in the future. Christ is still talking about that crucial point of pardon at the gates of heaven, or the time of final judgment from God.

Let a person profess that he is saved every day of his life: if his life does not demonstrate forgiving others, he will not be forgiven. It is true that no human being by effort can achieve such a life. By faith in Christ, humbly beseeching Christ for the power to forgive, living moment by moment in expectation of the Savior, and living in reflection of His deliverance of us, we forgive. Christ never said it would be easy. Much of His sermon is a pointer that we cannot reach heaven apart from Him being our righteousness, and so it is with forgiveness. We cannot forgive apart from Christ working in us.

But by Christ and through Christ, coming to know Him and His unfailing mercy to us, we are able to forgive. And this power to forgive is the power that assures us here, in this life, that our heavenly Father extends His forgiveness to us. When we see Him work in us to forgive, we know that He has also taken us in Hand and forgiven us, delighting to use us to glorify His power to forgive sinners.

Day Eighteen: Then came Peter to him, and said, Lord, how oft shall my brother sin against me, and I forgive him? till seven times?
Jesus saith unto him, I say not unto thee, Until seven times: but, Until seventy times seven.
Matthew 18:21-22

When Peter asked this famous question of the Lord, Peter already had been taught the nature and duty of forgiveness by Christ. He understood, and probably agreed overall, with the outlook of forgiveness that Christ taught. But there are those rare people we meet, who wrong us again and again. Like the rest of us, Peter was troubled by the hard cases: the people who don't stop hurting us. Peter reckoned that there must be some reasonable limit on the difficult task of forgiveness. At some point, we must be allowed to say that we have done enough, and now it is permissible to lash out, to strike back, to render evil for evil after we have tried our best to be kind. Peter wanted to count up the wrongs of his brother.

First, notice that Peter is talking about personal offenses. He is not talking about those criminal offenses that must be taken before governmental authority. But he is talking about a brother sinning against him. In the language of Peter's day, the word for brother in the original language could mean a fellow countryman, a fellow follower of Christ, or simply one's companion, like a neighbor or fellow laborer. Peter's question is not limited to those related to us by blood ties. Like many of us, Peter is seeking to know when forgiveness must stop, when he is free to no longer respect and care about the needs and life of one who wrongs him.

It is important to remember, that rebuke against offenses is commanded by the Lord Jesus as a means to bring about reconciliation (Luke 17:3). And offenses are to be brought before the elders if a person is unrepentant, as the Lord Jesus expressly commanded right before Peter brings forward this question. So forgiveness does not negate the need for rebuke, or even confrontation. But Christ tells us we must not hate, and we must always seek to restore and repair our broken relationships, even if the other person is entirely the offender. We must love the people who wrong us, and pray for them. And Peter wants to know when we are allowed to stop exercising ourselves to have compassion on those who wrong us.

The Lord Jesus' answer shows that counting up the wrongs of others is contrary to His teaching. He defines a number, seventy times seven, that indicates a point beyond counting. Immediately from this, the Lord goes into the story of the servant who is forgiven a great debt, who tries to punish his fellow servant for a tiny debt. The lesson is clear. Every day, we are forgiven our offenses. God forgives us beyond what any of us can count in terms of our offenses, and so we must forgive. We seek God in our troubles and griefs, and He forgives our sins so that He can hear us. And He expects the same from us: that when those who hurt us come begging for help and mercy, we must grant them help and mercy, forgiving their sins. We must not have an attitude of keeping count of the wrongs done by others.

And how can we do this? Like the rest of the Christian life, it is not possible except by faith in Christ, by living daily in terms of the reality of His full and free forgiveness, understanding that He has granted us heaven and acceptance with God. As we dwell upon what we have been given in Christ, it is possible, with our eyes on Christ, to forgive our enemies, to pray for them, and to hope for their good.

Day Nineteen: Judge not, and ye shall not be judged: condemn not, and ye shall not be condemned: forgive, and ye shall be forgiven:
Luke 6:37

This passage of Luke is part of a series of proverbs given by Christ: maxims to live by, as the proverbs of Solomon. We know from the teachings of the Lord Jesus that we as believers must exercise our sense of judgment, in the sense of discernment, when we hear teachers who claim to follow Christ. We must decide if they are telling the truth or not. John warns us to "try the spirits," to determine if they are of God. And the Bereans were commended for comparing the words of the apostles to the Scripture in order to reach a conclusion about them. So judgment in the sense of exercising discernment is not what Christ is talking about.

Christ is not saying that we must consent to wrongdoing on the grounds that we are also wrong doers. On the contrary, Christ tells us elsewhere to confront sin when sin offends and causes the innocent to stumble. The command to rebuke offenses as a means to reach reconciliation comes directly from Christ. We must recognize sin as sin, but we must also recognize our affinity and sameness with every other sinner.

The context of what Christ is saying here makes it clear. We must not judge others in the sense of condemning them from our hearts or thinking we have a right to hold a grudge. We are not to regard the sinner as less worthy than ourselves. We must approach all sin and all offenses with the recognition that our sins have been freely pardoned. We must not condemn out of hand, for we must sense that we ourselves could be condemned for our own sins. We must seek to forgive exactly because we seek forgiveness.

Christ previously warned His disciples in Matthew 5:22 that anybody who calls a person a "graceless wretch" is himself in danger of hellfire. And so we must take care to respect the throne of God and wait upon God's outcomes and God's judgments, and not presume to condemn in His name. Even in the book of I Corinthians, when Paul calls for the excommunication of a fornicating young man, Paul speaks in terms of delivering the young man to God for the final verdict. The church may expel based on the danger of open, brazen sin, but even the Christian church waits for God to condemn or save the soul.

Previously, we saw Christ speak in terms of our need for forgiveness when we stand before God for final judgment. But the passage in Luke is speaking in terms of our day to day relationship with God and our fellow man. The lifestyle of refusing to give up on those who harm us, of committing them into God's Hands instead of taking personal revenge, of praying for the people who harm us and representing them to God for mercy, bears its own fruit in this life.

Now, if you think about it, Christ Himself was unjustly judged, condemned, and killed for being a righteous man. He is not offering an iron clad escape from the injustices of this world with this proverbial statement. But He is affirming that the person who mourns for his own sin is comforted by God. The person who sincerely mourns over the sin of another is also comforted by God, for God Himself openly declares that He respects forgiveness. God, who declares Himself not a respecter of persons, does declare that He will regard those who forgive and thus wait upon Him for His final verdict.

Day Twenty: I pray thee, forgive the trespass of thine handmaid: for the LORD will certainly make my lord a sure house; because my lord fighteth the battles of the LORD, and evil hath not been found in thee all thy days. First Samuel chapter 25:28

Abigail was a person who had done no wrong in this passage. David, not yet crowned king and hunted by Saul, had quartered with his band of men among the sheepfolds in and around Hebron. David and his band were impoverished, hungry, and living in desperation. So their choice to stay among the shepherds in Hebron was wise for two reasons. First, the Philistines raided the Hebrews during harvest and at sheep shearing, and David's men could make themselves of service in protecting the flocks and the shepherds. Second, sheep shearing time was a time of celebration and generosity from the wealthy land owners to their laborers. David's presence, at face value, was a statement of expectation of some return for the protection that he and his men offered. Many vagrants came at sheep shearing to help in the daily work and participate in the feasting when all was finished.

And in this story in First Samuel chapter 25, the servants who cared for the sheep testified that David and his men were kind and just, and never stole a single lamb but protected sheep and men alike. Still, when David sent men to appeal to Nabal, a very wealthy landowner, Nabal violated the rules and expectations of hospitality and kindness of that culture. David's men came asking for food and water, a very humble request that put them as low as his lowest servants. David begged to be allowed to treat Nable as a father, a request that included an implicit guarantee of future protection of Nable. Yet Nable, when given a courteous and humble request that would have made a great man of him eventually, railed against David and his men. He sent them away in shame and disgrace, hurling insults and mockery after them, and he disdained their service to him in the fields. In a time of plenty, he denied them food and water.

Only recently, David had spared his greatest enemy, Saul. But now, enraged, David determined to kill Nabal and every man in Nable's household, even down to the children. This wrath was sin, and David's determination to kill was sin. But Nable's wife Abigail, alerted by a servant, gathered the very best of the food and wine and went to meet David and humbled herself before him and his men. Abigail's meekness and her commiseration with David for how he had been treated by her foolish husband quickly calmed David. And there is a reproof in her words, though she phrases it with great humility: "My Lord fighteth the battles of the Lord, and evil hath not been found in thee all thy days."

David himself stood on a precipice, always in danger of being slaughtered by Saul, and this cry for mercy from one about to suffer ruin from him brought him up short. In her extremity, Abigail even uttered a prophecy to David about his eventual victory and kingdom. In her humility, God was with her. And Abigail's cry for mercy was not just for herself. She acknowledged the churlish behavior of her husband but still begged for his life. She acknowledged David's standing before God and begged him to consider this before he threw it away in his anger. Abigail's wisdom is the wisdom of the person who places justice in the Hands of God. She recognized God's blessings upon David and appealed to God in her humble entreaty to David for mercy. In Abigail we see the quick measures of a believer to make peace and to restrain a man from committing gross sin. By her humility and wisdom, she preserved David, saved her own household, and even, indirectly, saw Nable brought to justice by the Hand of God.

Day Twenty-One: And David said to Abigail, Blessed be the LORD God of Israel, which sent thee this day to meet me: And blessed be thy advice, and blessed be thou, which hast kept me this day from coming to shed blood, and from avenging myself with mine own hand.
First Samuel chapter 25:32-33

With his armed men, swords on their belts, David was coming to avenge himself of the shameful way that Nabal had treated him and his men. Now, David had the promise of God that he would be king of Israel. And David had not wronged Nabal but had treated him honestly and with deference. But Nabal had wronged David and mocked him. And in the wilderness of Hebron, there was no power of justice or police to stop David from avenging his own honor.

As David marched towards Nabal's home, David was telling himself that he had a right to kill Nabal and every male of Nabal's household. And yet David was the man who had forgiven and spared Saul only recently, the wicked king who unjustly sought to kill him! But the affront of Nabal had been unexpected to David, a shocking insult and outrage from a man of no real political importance. And when David received the shock of Nabal's sin against him, David reacted from injured pride and his own sense of outrage.

In today's passage, David's words to Abigail are telling in his open confession of the wrongness of what he had been about to do. David blesses Abigail because she prevented him from shedding blood. He declares her *blessed*, that is, one who is allowed to kneel before God, a woman favored of God: cherished by God and adorned with His goodness. And he acknowledges that her advice is also blessed. That is, the decision to not shed blood is a decision that is favored of God, and those who hold to such decisions are those favored of God and allowed to make their supplications to Him under His favor.

David publicly rejects his previous thinking and declares that seeking to avenge himself was contrary to the blessed estate.   He regards Abigail's intervention as his salvation, a blessing that keeps him in the privileged place as a supplicant acceptable to God. If David had avenged himself, he would have endangered his favored place with God.

Today in Christianity, some men try to make Christianity a warlike, aggressive religion, all in the name of avenging ourselves. But while Christian integrity demands lawful and just behavior, there is no room at the feet of Christ for vigilante justice or a delight in killing our enemies. There are men who climb into pulpits and breathe out their wrath against unbelievers and criminals. And yet it is noteworthy that, for all their wrathful speaking, they effect no beneficial change. They fail to comfort the afflicted, and all their wrath and proud boasting of the violence they wish upon others fails to hold evil in check. Indeed, some who have strutted in their wrath against evil have been found silently endorsing it when conditions favored their silence.

David learned early not to avenge himself. And forgiveness itself is the act, not of saying that evil is acceptable, because it isn't, but of putting the evil that others do to us into the hands of lawful authority; And ultimately, when even human law fails, into God's Hands. At its root, forgiveness is an act of faith in God, the ultimate action of expressing trust in Him.

Day Twenty-Two: Take heed to yourselves: If thy brother trespass against thee, rebuke him; and if he repent, forgive him.
Luke 17:3

Today's verse comes from a passage in Luke where the Lord Jesus is not so much entreating us to forgive, but rather warning us of the dangers of offending. "Offenses will come," He tells his disciples in verse 1 of this chapter, "But woe unto him through whom they come!" And then He tells His followers to take heed to themselves and rebuke those who offend them.

Many readers of the Bible recognize that Christ is allowing us to rebuke those who wrong us. We have a right to tell a person who has wronged us exactly what he or she has done that caused us harm or grief. And Christ continues further in this passage in Luke 17 to say that as often as the same person offends us, we are to rebuke that person. If he repents, we forgive again. If he offends again, we rebuke again.

But Christ is not only giving His people the right to rebuke when they are wronged. He is affirming that because offenses are certain from sinners, and because God punishes offenders, we are to take heed to ourselves. That is, we are to act to preserve our offending brothers by rebuking them. The type of rebuke that Christ describes is a rebuke founded on the fear of God and His just chastening and wrath.

The Lord has just taught that those who offend the innocent shall suffer dire punishment, and He follows this decree with the warning that we must take heed. That is, we have to be careful and meticulous. For the sake of all

Christendom, and for the sake of our brothers who offend, and even for our own sakes, we are to rebuke offenses. The transaction that Christ describes here is simple, straightforward, and painless. We may not take revenge, We are not to rail or accuse. We are not even to condemn. But we are to declare the offense and its wrongness. And this is done with the end goal of pardon and reconciliation in mind. The moment our brother repents, we forgive.

Christ here lays down a pattern of behavior that preserves all Christendom. Unrebuked corruption and sin will undo us corporately, and not just individually. The goal of rebuke is to reconcile and pardon. In offering rebuke, we offer our brothers and sisters the opportunity to be reconciled and forgiven. We know from other passages that rebuke is to be private and kind hearted. We also know that rebuke itself can be escalated and made progressively more public, if repentance and reconciliation are not possible. Rebuke can be turned over to the elders, for them to rule on a grievance. And all of this is done with the hope of restoration, reconciliation, and pardon in mind.

We are guilty of trespasses, and so we must extend forgiveness to those who trespass against us, and rebuke itself is a means to reconciliation. But the act of rebuking a person biblically is an action designed to preserve our brother and ourselves from the dangers of committing offenses that will bring God's displeasure upon us. How rightly Christ warns us to "take heed," for we are all sinners, and we must help each other in the proper fear of God and the in hope of is forgiveness.

Day Twenty-Three: Surely at the commandment of the LORD came [this] upon Judah, to remove [them] out of his sight, for the sins of Manasseh, according to all that he did; And also for the innocent blood that he shed: for he filled Jerusalem with innocent blood; which the LORD would not pardon.
Second Kings 24:3 and 4

It is possible to overtax the kindness of a merciful God. And it is possible to affront God, the God who became a man in order to forgive our sin, to the point that He does not forgive. Nor is every sin merely an individual matter. Human beings are social creatures, and a society of human beings can commit national sins. A congregation of a church can commit corporate sins.

The bible says Manasseh had sinned beyond the sins of those countries that the Lord had destroyed before the Israelites. Indeed, a quick review of his evil deeds shows a delight in him in affronting the religion of the Israelites and profaning the God of Israel. He sacrificed his own children to pagan gods, and he persecuted the faithful Israelites who held fast to their faith. Jewish tradition holds that it was Manasseh who killed the prophet Isaiah. But Manasseh could not commit his sins in a vacuum. In his day, there were religious leaders who went one way to please him in his evil, and immediately turned another way to please him when he repented.

Judah was guilty of national sin. Her religious leaders, as Isaiah had so plainly mourned, were false and unrepentant. When the king called for the deaths of the innocent, they drew up the papers and sent the agents to shed blood. When the king repented his evil deeds, they commiserated with him, with an eye to keeping themselves in his favor. God granted Manasseh a reprieve, for Manasseh did repent. His grandson Josiah likewise repented of the idolatry of the nation, and God promised Josiah peace during his lifetime.

But the death of the faithful and the innocent was not mourned in Judah. The prophets Isaiah and Jeremiah alike lamented the gross indifference and wickedness of the religious leaders. Many had forgotten or neglected to teach that true professors had been martyred under Manasseh. People assumed that God no longer cared about His abused and murdered saints. But time does not dull the justice of God. And a reprieve is not a pardon. For the sake of the godly, He spared Judah to the fourth generation, but as He has warned in His Word, He returned His wrath upon that city for its evil.

The great grandson of Manasseh, Jehoiakim, saw the wrath of God fall when the King of Babylon subjected Judah. But even then, the Lord's wrath did not abate, for the king and the noble families continued in their pride and in their sins against the poor and innocent. In the end, the royal lines of Judah were taken captive or killed. Much of Jerusalem was deported, and only the poor were left behind, to reap the vineyards of the wealthy. The Babylonians favored the prophet Jeremiah and those who had protected him. But the city was burned, the temple destroyed, most of the people carried away captive. And this warning remains to us: that we must not regard old evil as forgotten evil. We must repent of sin, including corporate sin. Yes, we are stained by what our nation does. We are stained by what our church does.

God forgives, but God is also the God of justice. He avenges the innocent. And he avenges His people. His wrath may remain silent for four generations, but when God executes justice, there is no escape. It is a dangerous error to assume that God forgets about sin, or that the suffering and death of the very least of His brethren should escape His concern to impose His justice.

Day Twenty-Four: Their land also is full of idols; they worship the work of their own hands, that which their own fingers have made:
the mean man boweth down, and the great man humbleth himself: therefore forgive them not.
Isaiah 2:8-9

Some translators believe that this verse should be rendered this way in English: the mean man boweth down, and the great man humbleth himself: *And thou wilt not forgive them.* Either way, the meaning is clear and dreadful. It is possible to sin away the day of Grace. Isaiah looked upon a nation where both the small and impoverished and the rich and mighty bowed down to false gods. Isaiah cannot find the name of righteousness in the land. It is true that from Isaiah's time to our time, individuals of any country have repented of sin. Isaiah is describing the condemnation of a nation as an entity. Some few godly individuals would escape by repentance, but the nation would be unforgiven and given over to wrath.

This passage is describing the need for corporate repentance: the repentance of a federated group of people, like a nation, or a church. And Isaiah's condemnation is just. For this nation had been chosen of God for blessing from the outset. They had many true witnesses of God's deliverance of them. God had given them, and only them, His Law, and His prophets. He had given them His chastening and His restoration. He had proved Himself faithful to His Word. And yet the nation abandoned Him. They paid lip service to Him, but they openly broke His Law, oppressed the poor, and lived for money and affluence.

The Lord Jesus, the Master who taught forgiveness and lived forgiveness, also expressed this dreadful verdict upon cities, when He proclaimed, "Woe unto thee, Chorazin! woe unto thee, Bethsaida! for if the mighty works had been done in Tyre and Sidon, which have been done in you, they had a great while ago repented, sitting in sackcloth and ashes. But it shall be more tolerable for Tyre and Sidon at the judgment, than for you. And thou, Capernaum, which art exalted to heaven, shalt be thrust down to hell."

Whoever receives the light of God's gracious enlightenment and ignores it, or darkens it with corruption, is in terrible danger. And any corporate entity, such as a nation, or a church, who perverts God's grace and righteousness, and harms the innocent, and fails to repent, is in danger of losing the day of grace.

Isaiah condemns the nation but urges the individuals to humble themselves. He writes, "Enter into the rock, and hide thee in the dust, for fear of the LORD, and for the glory of his majesty." And he makes a dreadful promise: "The lofty looks of man shall be humbled, and the haughtiness of men shall be bowed down, and the LORD alone shall be exalted in that day. For the day of the LORD of hosts [shall be] upon every [one that is] proud and lofty, and upon every [one that is] lifted up; and he shall be brought low." Isaiah chapter 2, verses 10 through 12. The great danger of pride is its blindness. Those who pride themselves on anything within themselves, and those who trust in anything they have made, are doomed. There comes a point where some cannot repent and they hate repentance. But whoever humbles himself or herself before the righteousness of God finds forgiveness and grace, and is spared.

Day Twenty-Five: And why dost thou not pardon my transgression, and take away mine iniquity? for now shall I sleep in the dust; and thou shalt seek me in the morning, but I shall not be.
Job 7:21

One great error concerning forgiveness, is to sin away the day of Grace. But the opposite error also exists: to suppose that God harbors a grievance against us when He does not. It can be a mistake to think suffering is a chance thing. We should always inspect our suffering with a mind to humble ourselves before it. And yet, not all suffering comes to us as punishment for sin.

Poor Job, a godly and a wise man, had lost all his children, all his household, all his possessions. And then he had lost his health. His wife blamed him, assuming that these calamities had come upon them because of something evil Job had done. In her despair, she calls upon him to curse God and die, am exclamation that may indicate that she thought Job had undertaken some sort of great offense to God, for which there was no remedy. Job's counselors had come to advise him to repent. But Job could not find any sin he had committed that would have reaped such catastrophic punishment.

Ultimately, Job pleads himself a sinner, as all men are sinners. He acknowledges his need for God's forgiveness, daily. Indeed, when Job had owned livestock, Job had sought the Lord daily, with sacrifices, to atone for his sins and the sins of his family. His entire life was a statement that he needed and had faith in God's power to reconcile him to God by grace.

And so, at this point in the book of Job, Job laments that God has declined to pardon him. Job attributes his suffering to his sinful estate, and to God's indignation against him as a sinner. But the truth is, God had decreed the afflictions of Job precisely because God had made a claim of Job's integrity and faithfulness to Him before all the witness of Heaven. God had backed Job to Satan himself. In a sense, we could say that God had staked His own reputation upon a mere man, upon Job. God honored Job.

The mental anguish of Job was not the least of his sufferings, for Job mistakenly feared that the redemption he had in God was now abandoned by God. Nor did Job rebel at this. He humbled himself and pleaded with God to accept him again on the grounds of God's mercy. From the beginning of this book, Job indicates a certain expectation that his life was ending. And here, in chapter 7, he begs God to simply end it: to forgive him and let him die. Poor Job did not know that his life was only at its halfway point, and that God planned to deck him with joy and honor all his days, and to restore family, possessions, health, and joy to him.

It is right, when we are afflicted, to humble ourselves before God and prayerfully consider His purposes and confess our sins. But it is a mistake to think that affliction indicates that God has abandoned us or does not care about us. God dwells among those who are contrite and humble, to revive them, according to Isaiah chapter 57. He chastens those He loves. He lets us bear reproach so that He can rebuke the world for its sin.

It is wise and right to walk humbly with God, ready to receive His correction and instruction. But we must remember that God does not abandon the redemption that He offers to those who trust in Him.

Day Twenty-Six: Look upon mine affliction and my pain; and forgive all my sins. Consider mine enemies; for they are many; and they hate me with cruel hatred. Keep my soul, and deliver me: let me not be ashamed; for I put my trust in thee.
Psalms 25:18-20

When David prayed, he did not make a distinction between spiritual well being and physical or material well being. He brought his entire condition to God for remedy and help. David saw himself as a unified whole: a person in need of God's protection, healing, and forgiveness. David recognizes in this Psalm, in fact, that sin is both the source of all his other failings, as well as the outcome of his estate as a frail and fallen creature upon this earth. He begs God to look upon his affliction and pain, but notice that he doesn't ask for specific remedies directed at affliction and pain. Instead, he begs for God to consider his suffering and therefore, to forgive his sins.

It is true that some people today oversimplify the link between sin and suffering and suppose that each illness can be cured if you can only identify the sin that caused it and get forgiveness. David isn't buying into that notion. But he is praying in terms of his sinful estate being the root of distress in his life.

In this Psalm, David confesses his estate: afflicted, suffering, sinful: beset with enemies, and threatened with shame. But his supplication is, first, for forgiveness of his sins. In this Psalm, David foresees what Paul the Apostle would later write with great detail: that the redemption of God offers cleansing from sin but also a gracious estate of being found pleasing to God. By humility and repentance, the believer enters the covenant of God's favor. God favors

His beloved people, not because they deserve His favor, but because He has chosen to grant them His favor.

David never pleads his own worthiness in this Psalm. He pleads for God's mercy based on the merciful attribute of God. David is not bargaining but rather begging. But God hears beggars. Christ Himself taught that, first and foremost, the poor in spirit inherit the Kingdom of heaven. Those who beg from God are given His inheritance.

Next, David's only standing is that He trusts in God. He was a king and he was given a place of honor among the mighty men of Israel. But David didn't value these achievements at all when he stood before God. His trust in God was all he had to claim, and this, again, was actually a claim on God's promise to deliver those who trust in Him: a promise founded on God's mercy and not our ability to do better or to earn mercy.

Finally, David lays his entire condition before God. In contrast to what many people today teach, David didn't go to God for forgiveness and then leave it to himself to out think and out maneuver his enemies. He lays his entire condition before God: Trusting in God to forgiven his sin, he also trusts God to keep him from being a prey to his enemies and from suffering the shame of coming under their power. David doesn't quite ask God to deliver him from all pain and affliction. He simply reminds God of the weight of his earthly condition. But he does specifically ask that he not be abandoned to those who hate him. In this Psalm, David recognizes the need to come begging for forgiveness from God, but he also recognizes that having the right to come, confessing sin, he is also given the right to lay every other trouble before God and to hope in God for deliverance and protection.

Day Twenty-Seven: But he held his peace, and answered nothing. Again the high priest asked him, and said unto him, Art thou the Christ, the Son of the Blessed? Jesus said, I am: and ye shall see the Son of man sitting on the right hand of power, and coming in the clouds of heaven. Mark chapter 14:61-62

When Christ was put to death, there were three events that evoked forgiveness from Him. And each transaction of forgiveness was slightly different from the others. Today's passage shows the first of the three transactions of forgiveness.

Forgiveness itself is not the same thing as excusing sin or ignoring sin. In fact, it's impossible to forgive sin without both offender and offended understanding, with at least some level of mutual understanding, exactly what the offense was. Forgiveness is the pardon of sin, as far as a person can pardon sin. Furthermore, forgiveness is the act of taking our hands off of a wrong done to us and committing that wrong into God's Hands. Ideally, forgiveness demonstrates faith in God by reinstating a grieving loved one to his or her previous happy estate with us, with all wrongs resolved and forgotten.

But reinstatement isn't always possible. As we see in today's passage, there are people who hate us whether we have been kind to them or not. There are people who do evil to others because doing evil is in their own best interest to secure their own power and prosperity. When Christ was brought before the Sanhedrin in their quickly convened and secret meeting, He knew that they had convened expressly to condemn Him. He also knew that they knew that He had fulfilled the writings of the Prophets, and that they recognized that He certainly could be the Messiah, but He was not the political, powerful Messiah they had expected.

What the Pharisees and Sadducees did to Christ, they did with full knowledge that their actions were evil, and that He was innocent. And so when He was asked the question that was designed to condemn Him, Christ answered with the name of God, "I AM," a clear statement of His Godhood. He didn't rant and rave at the Sanhedrin. He simply told them with terse and straightforward clarity what their own end would be: they would see Him coming at the right Hand of power in the clouds of heaven. a prediction of the destruction of Jerusalem and their final destruction on earth. He didn't say it gleefully or with relish. He simply said it: their last warning before they condemned themselves in the terrible thing they were about to do to the Son of God.

Before men who were willing to commit a great atrocity with full knowledge of its evil and full recognition that the Law of God forbade them to do such a thing, Christ still committed His plight to God. He did not hate His killers, and He did tell them the dreadful truth that awaited them. The only kind thing Christ could do for the Sanhedrin was warn them of the wrath they were piling up for themselves. So He told them.

Before those who knowingly and willingly killed Him, Christ was steadfast in maintaining the truth and in offering them a final warning, a chance to escape committing this great sin, even a warning that some would take away and ponder. But Christ committed the matter to God, and He put Himself in God's Hands. When nothing on earth could save Him from the sins of those who willingly did evil to Him, Christ did not engage in carnal warfare. He committed Himself to God, treated His killers with honesty and dignity, and maintained the truth.

Day Twenty-Eight: And one of the malefactors which were hanged railed on him, saying, "If thou be Christ, save thyself and us." But the other answering rebuked him, saying, "Dost not thou fear God, seeing thou art in the same condemnation? And we indeed justly; for we receive the due reward of our deeds: but this man hath done nothing amiss." And he said unto Jesus, "Lord, remember me when thou comest into thy kingdom." And Jesus said unto him, "Verily I say unto thee, To day shalt thou be with me in paradise."
Luke chapter 23:39-43

When Christ was put to death, there were three events that evoked forgiveness from Him. And each transaction of forgiveness was slightly different from the others. Today's passage shows the second of the three transactions of forgiveness on the day Christ died.

Previously, we saw that when the Lord Jesus stood before men who knew they were doing wrong and did it anyway, He did not rail against them or berate them. He declared Himself as the Christ, and He forthrightly told them of the destruction they would eventually suffer from God's Hand. But His words were spare and terse: a warning and a guarantee, but not a threat to manipulate them. Truly, Christ was offering them the only thing He could offer: a final chance to repent and reject their own plan to kill Him.

In today's passage, we see Christ confronted by the opposite: a sinner who frankly confesses that the sentence against him is just, and who likewise confesses that Christ is an innocent and a Godly man, who ought to have been spared this type of death. This poor thief makes a dying request of Christ, to receive mercy from Him when Christ enters His kingdom.

Now, it is entirely likely that this poor condemned man did not even comprehend the theology of Jesus Christ. He addresses Christ as Lord, but he speaks nothing of the Messiah. He calls the kingdom of God "thy kingdom" to Christ, a possible reflection of the fact that he knew about this kingdom only from what He was hearing the rabble throw at Christ in their insults and jibes against Him.

However much he did or did not understand, it is clear that the dying thief did not have the enlightenment of Scripture that the Pharisees had. But he did have Christ before him, and he knew, from what he saw of Christ, that the very way that Christ endured the cross, praying for His enemies, comforting the women who mourned over His death, that this man Jesus was not like any other man who had ever walked on the face of the earth. In his plea, the dying thief stood upon the same ground that David stood upon in so many of his prayers in the Psalms: the thief had no righteousness to claim. He even denounced himself for all the evil he had done. But the basis of his plea is the graciousness and kindness he saw of Christ while Christ hung on the cross. The thief made a bold request, to be forgiven and accepted into the very same circle of the mysterious kingdom where Christ was going. And what emboldened him was Christ before him, gracious and compassionate even in the pains of a slow and torturous death.

And Christ made a bold answer of free grace: that the thief would have fellowship with Him that same day in Paradise. So when Christ, even with all He was suffering on the cross, heard the plea for forgiveness from one who may not have perfectly understood Christ but loved Him and hoped in Him, Christ boldly and utterly forgave the man and granted him the estate of heaven.

Some people think that detailed and accurate knowledge of theology saves us. But while doctrine is essential, to love Christ and hope in Him, having faith in Him, is all that repentance needs to find peace with Christ.

Day Twenty-Nine: Then said Jesus, Father, forgive them; for they know not what they do. And they parted his raiment, and cast lots.
Luke 23:34

When Christ was put to death, there were three events that evoked forgiveness from Him. And each transaction of forgiveness was slightly different from the others. Today's passage shows the last of the three transactions of forgiveness on the day Christ died.

We have seen previously that the Sanhedrin knowingly killed Christ, and they did not want His forgiveness. Christ committed Himself to God when under their power, and He warned them of the danger of what they were doing. To the dying and repentant thief, Christ granted a full and free pardon, the promise of fellowship with Him in Paradise.

And finally, as Christ hung upon the Cross, He had the torment of watching men totally indifferent to His suffering and death squabble over His few possessions and gamble to see who would win His cloak. The Romans came from a culture that did not value all human life. Romans valued strength and courage. In Roman society, a father had the right to kill his own child if it were deformed or simply did not please him in any way. In Rome, only the strong survived.

To Romans, those who committed capital offenses were worth killing off: people less worthy than themselves, drains upon the empire. The Roman soldiers who executed Christ regarded their work as mere business. They made a small profit from dividing up the last possessions of the condemned. That was all Christ was to them: a dirty job and a chance to get some free clothing. These men were witness to the indignities that Christ suffered. They saw Him pray for His enemies as H e was dying. They saw Him remain silent when harassed and mocked. They heard the women lament over the miracles Christ had done for others. They simply didn't care. They didn't believe He was the Son of God. To the Romans, the idea of one single God was foreign and strange. And their gods seemed to be doing much better than the God of the Jews, in their opinion.

They did not respect human life as the prophets had taught respect for human life. They did not respect the God of the Jews. They thought themselves to be superior, nationally, to Judeans. And they certainly believed, individually, that each one of them was a better man than any condemned man hanging on a Cross. In short, the Romans who killed Christ, and even the many people who begged Him with tears to come down from the Cross and then flew into outrage when He did not come down, did not understand who Christ was. It can be argued that what they did, howling their anger at Him while He suffered, or mocking Him, or callously dividing up His clothing as their reward, was still wrong and was still sin. But Christ, even when dying and suffering their wrong doing, granted as much grace to them as He could give. He prayed for God to spare them from God's indignation, because they did not comprehend the enormity of their own sin.

For men who had the enlightenment of the Scripture and were still hard hearted, Christ had made no such prayer. He had submitted to them in God's Will, and warned them. But for these who thought there was a legitimate grievance against Him, Christ prayed for them to be forgiven. As He had done with those who knowingly wronged Him, Christ committed these sinners and their sins against Him to

God, but with a prayer for mercy for them. This also is forgiveness. If we cannot reinstate people to fellowship with us, we can pray for them to receive merciful treatment from God. Christ has prayed for us, and we are to imitate Him and pray for those who, by their weakness, are alienated from us.

Day Thirty: And they shall teach no more every man his neighbour, and every man his brother, saying, Know the LORD: for they shall all know me, from the least of them unto the greatest of them, saith the LORD: for I will forgive their iniquity, and I will remember their sin no more.
Jeremiah 31:34

The writer of the Book of Hebrews in the New Testament re-iterates the entire passage of Jeremiah 31:31-34, including this crucial verse. When the people of Israel were brought into the dust by God, taken captive for the guilt of their sins, removed from their beloved land, witness to the burning of their city, Jerusalem, they truly felt the weight, not only of their sin, but of the great alienation they had caused between themselves and God. They mourned over their sin then, but it was too late, and their tears and prayers didn't turn them back from captivity in a strange land, among their triumphant enemies.

Jeremiah's ministry changed from one of condemnation and warning, to one of tenderness and hope. And through him, God uttered a promise that changed the world: A new covenant, not the old covenant that God had made when He brought His people out of Egypt, but a covenant founded in the righteousness of God Himself, lived out on behalf of His people, would offer even greater grace to sinners. The political nation of Israel might fail, but the children of the promise would be counted as the seed of Israel, a nation born, not of flesh, but of the Spirit. These are the children spoken of in Romans chapter nine, the Israel of God. Jeremiah foretold them, his prophecy of this spiritual seed sealed by its inclusion in the book of Hebrews, where the writer asserts that the new covenant of

Jesus Christ has done away with the former covenant given to Moses.

Under the covenant of Christ, the new covenant, or New Testament, we are given an abundance of knowledge of God. And the Lord our Righteousness, Jesus Christ, has lived among us, taught us, and left with us the Advocate, the Holy Spirit. Under the blessed covenant of Grace, God has called forth His people from every nation, and He has forgiven our sins.

The people of God are now sealed to God by a spiritual transaction, through Jesus Christ our High Priest. God has undertaken to be the righteousness of His people, and to represent them and minister to them as their faithful High Priest. In the new covenant promised by Jeremiah, we are given righteousness in Christ, and our sins are forgiven. This is our hope, not to hope in ourselves, but to humbly come before God with hope in our Savior Jesus Christ.

Printed in Great Britain
by Amazon